BRITAIN'S HERITAGE

Industrial Railways

Anthony Coulls

AMBERLEY

Acknowledgements

My thanks for this volume to James West, James Wells and Daniel Teale for specific images to fill in parts of the story. All other photographs are by the author or Peter Coulls, to whom I also thank for engendering my interest in industrial railways from an early age.

Dedicated to Fred Coulls, an industrial locomotive driver who ensured that my dad's birth certificate had 'Profession of Father – Engine Driver' on it.

Cover image: Taken by the author, showing locomotives with a torpedo wagon at Scunthorpe steelworks in July 2021.

First published 2022

Amberley Publishing
The Hill, Stroud
Gloucestershire, GL5 4EP

www.amberley-books.com

Copyright © Anthony Coulls, 2022

The right of Anthony Coulls to be identified as the Author of this work has been asserted in accordance with the Copyrights, Designs and Patents Act 1988.

ISBN 978 1 4456 9862 5 (paperback)
ISBN 978 1 4456 9863 2 (ebook)

British Library Cataloguing in Publication Data.
A catalogue record for this book is available from the British Library.

Typesetting by SJmagic DESIGN SERVICES, India.
Printed in the UK.

Contents

1

What is an Industrial Railway?

Away from the glamour of the main-line express, thousands of miles of industrial railway moved raw materials and finished products from the very dawn of railways in the UK. From sewage works to sugar factory, all manner of industries were served, employing on occasion dozens of locomotives or in other cases simply a horse or a petrol tractor. The Beckton gasworks in London ran a massive railway, complete with locomotive roundhouse and signals, while the ironstone industry of the East Midlands operated on the edge of fields. Truly it can be said that one was never more than a mile or two from an industrial railway, even if one didn't know or realise it existed. Cable-worked lines abounded in town brickworks, and a cornucopia of locomotives provided power, while a fantastic array of specialist wagons moved all manner of goods, some of them hardly salubrious! A few industrial lines have survived to be kept as heritage attractions; one is even a Scheduled Ancient Monument. Part of the book looks at these heritage lines, as well as the ways in which you can find out more about them and their history or even become a spare time coal train driver. For the purposes of keeping the book to a reasonable length, we'll mainly concentrate on what are now understood as standard gauge railways. Narrow gauge lines are no less important to the

The modern industrial railway is seen well in this image of a Hunslet diesel loco passing through the Scunthorpe steelworks complex in July 2021.

railway story of the British Isles but are covered more comprehensively in the companion volume in this series *Narrow Gauge Locomotives*.

The concept of a railway has been around for centuries. The eminent railway historian Dr Michael Lewis defined a railway as 'a prepared tracks that support a wheeled vehicle and where guidance is supplied by the interface between the track and the wheel'. In other words, the purpose of the railway is to reduce friction between a vehicle and the ground to allow a larger load to be carried than is possible with human or animal carriage alone. Wood on wood gave way to iron on iron and eventually steel on steel. Each time, the rolling resistance is lowered, and a greater payload becomes possible. The concept of a railway as above has been around since classical times, often in domestic or theatrical settings. The Diolkos way in Greece across the Pelopponese, while only a few miles in length and constructed in stone, was in operation for nearly seven centuries from 600 BC. It was used for moving boats across the isthmus rather than taking the treacherous and longer sea voyage around the coast.

Whether or not you accept the concept as a railway, the idea was proven and has been around for over two and a half millennia. In the UK, the railway was introduced in a very small way into the copper and lead mines of Cumbria in the sixteenth century. Georgius Agricola wrote the classic *De Re Metallica* in the 1500s, depicting mining methods and technology in Germany and including wooden railways and wagons. These were known as 'hund' trucks due to the noise made by the guide pins between the two wooden rails – a bit like an ancient slot car, the Scalextric of its day. The mining technology entered England with German miners in mid-sixteenth century and in the last twenty years, mine explorers found real remains of these railways and had the timber dated to verify their age. Amazingly this pointed to a date in the 1560s – the oldest surviving railway in the British Isles. Not in the industrial heartlands of the Midlands, North East or South Wales, but in the Cumbrian Fells, where silver lead could be found and was worked. Small scale it might have been, but the significance of the railway coming to the British Isles was to have an impact on centuries of transport in the future. The wagons were pushed by miners, with a capacity of no more than two or three wheelbarrows' worth, and while the remains on site are now vestigial in the form of rails and sleepers, a replica hund is displayed in the Great Hall of the National Railway Museum. The original site remains inaccessible to all but the most determined and hardy.

> The 'hund' came directly from the German, as in 'dog' because the sound of wood on wood made a sort of barking noise.

An industrial railway can be defined as one that serves any industry of any size and is not a common carrier public railway. Moving timber in a woodyard on a couple of narrow gauge trucks by hand is just as much an industrial railway as the several miles of double-track railway from the ironstone quarries in Northamptonshire serving the Corby steelworks – both were built for a specific purpose, whereas a public railway is open to carry all goods and passengers. Not that it can be said that industrial railways did not carry passengers – many did, and repurposed old main line carriages to do so – and we shall return to those in due course. They even ran a timetabled service, but were mainly doing so for workers engaged in the industries they served, and fitted between the trains of goods such as coal

Hand-pushed mine wagons are depicted in this frieze in the Russian Ethnographic Museum in St Petersburg, showing how the concept of railways was universal.

on the Ashington system in the North East of England. In between, sand pits, scrapyards and soap works all relied on the industrial railway to enable them to continue with their particular enterprises. Track gauges varied from very narrow to broader than Brunel's broad gauge, but for this book's purposes, the focus will be on what became the standard gauge.

2

Down to the Sea in Trucks – Wooden Waggonways and After

It wasn't long after the introduction of railed transport in the mines that the technology made its way to the surface and grew in scale. Not being confined in tunnels, the rail gauge grew, wagons got larger, and horses were introduced to pull wagons – and they could manage longer trains too. The first recorded above ground railway of any length in Britain was in Nottinghamshire, where Huntingdon Beaumont built a line from his coal mines on his estate at Strelley. This was in 1603, over 200 years before the first steam locomotive. From here, the concept of the railway began to spread and found favour in coal mining areas. In parallel development with canals, initially the canal network grew further and faster while the railways remained at shorter distances around pitheads and at wharves. Rails were wood, speeds were low and loads relatively light.

By the eighteenth century, the wooden railway had spread to Shropshire, then South Wales and the North East of England. Networks of dozens of miles crossed the landscape, and initially were known as waggonways. Even now, parts of County Durham show the legacy of miles of railway, closed well over a century before the famous Beeching cuts of the 1960s, as earthworks remain in the landscape. It is in the waggonways of the North East that the origins of what became standard gauge – 4 feet, 8.5 inches between the rails – became clear in the 1770s. A remarkable find in the early twenty-first century was an incredibly well-preserved section of wooden railway on the north bank of the River Tyne – the Willington waggonway. Excavation and research of this led by Richard Carlton and Les Turnbull has given a remarkable insight into not just the technical make-up and operation of these railways, but an understanding of just how much the networks made up arteries of industry, from the collieries to the ships. With an intensive operation of a wagon each way every two minutes, with few passing places, and running to service a tidal river where boats were limited to how long they could load – and all this without telephone or internet communication – the undertaking must have been impressive indeed. Far from the impression that some railway histories give that these early railways were slow and bucolic. Local they may have been geographically, but in terms of activity and importance they laid the foundations for networks in decades to come.

Wooden rails gave way to iron rails: plateways at first, then the use of edge rails with flanged wheels but the horse remained in charge. Then all changed with the young steam engineer Richard Trevithick, from Cornwall. He set the path for the next development of the railway – that of enhancing the existing industrial steam engine, which allowed the miniaturisation of the technology and arguably set its path for even greater world

Above: The Willington Waggonway was an amazing find on the north bank of the River Tyne and led to in-depth research into its origins and operation. Parts of it were saved by Tyne & Wear Museums and the National Railway Museum.

Below: At Blists Hill Museum, part of the Ironbridge complex of sites, is a 1990s-built replica of the locomotive thought to have been built in Coalbrookdale by Richard Trevithick. Whether such an engine existed is now doubtful, but early industrial railways in Shropshire were very much a reality.

domination. Trevithick experimented with higher pressure in his boilers and engines, calling it 'strong steam'. He went to Coalbrookdale in Shropshire in 1802, where the Coalbrookdale Company made the first commercial high-pressure boilers and perhaps later the first steam railway locomotive – there already being several early railway systems in the county and in the Dale in particular.

The use of higher pressure also increased the risk of boiler explosions, leading steam power pioneer James Watt to protest strongly, suggesting that Trevithick 'deserved to be hung'. Trevithick responded by going somewhere where his experience and ability were welcomed and encouraged: South Wales. In an 1804 bet with a local ironmaster, William Homfray, he built a steam locomotive to run on the Penydarren tramroad to pull wagons to the Merthyr canal and in so doing laid the seeds for the steam locomotive's development and ultimate displacement of the horse – though this would never be fully eclipsed on the railway scene. He made smaller high-pressure engines for transport purposes and stationary power applications. There was a similarity between the designs, and one of his stationary engines was put into a boat. Later, some of the Trevithick engines built by the Hazeldine Company at Bridgnorth in Shropshire bore very striking similarities to the 1808 locomotive *Catch Me Who Can* built to run on a circular track in London.

> The horse as a source of motive power on the railways of Britain lasted from 1603 to 1999, long before and after the steam locomotive. Perhaps appropriately the first and last use was in moving coal from small mines.

While initially the high weight of the locomotive compared to the brittle iron rails meant a slow start, the steam locomotive was rapidly developed, and the high cost of feeding horses around the time of the Napoleonic Wars saw technological advances that would change the face of the British railway. Starting with the Middleton Railway in Leeds with the first commercially successful steam locomotives of the Blenkinsop pattern, it wasn't long before the eminent engineer George Stephenson of Wylam was experimenting and observing the locomotives of William Hedley and then creating his own machines.

No full-size Blenkinsop locomotives survived the nineteenth century, but a contemporary model and a reproduction rack wheel made from an original pattern were displayed in the National Railway Museum and Science Museum's exhibition 'Brass, Steel and Fire' between 2019 and 2021.

The original *Puffing Billy* of William Hedley is shown in the Science Museum, London. Beamish Museum in County Durham have a full-scale working replica, which in April 2017 was operated on the recreated colliery railway at the museum to give an impression of the earliest steam worked lines.

By this time, the concept of the publicly funded common carrier railway had taken off, along with passenger travel for all. In 1825, the first public railway designed to use steam traction from the outset opened – the Stockton & Darlington Railway, its motto 'Private Enterprise for Public Good'. Before long, Britain was in the grip of a railway mania, and commercially funded companies began to build longer networks of railways for all. It's here that the industrial railway began to carve its own identity – serving the public system on whatever scale was appropriate, feeding in coal, timber and stone to the national network for onward distribution. Private sidings serving a small industrial concern or factory or a full private line of several miles, if they didn't serve a common carrying purpose, were to all intents and purposes an industrial railway. Small lines grew off the Stockton & Darlington Railway, such as the Surtees Railway, serving collieries on the other side of the town of Shildon in County Durham. As the nineteenth century progressed, larger systems came into being, such as the Lambton, Pensnett and Wemyss Railways all carrying coal, or the dozens of miles of railways built around the Staffordshire town of Burton upon Trent, to supply raw materials and distribute the products of the brewing industry.

In 1822, the Hetton Railway was opened to move coal in County Durham. Nearly thirty years later a new locomotive *Lyon* was made, which copied the original Stephenson type but also incorporated modern materials and technology for the time. It can now be seen at Locomotion Museum in Shildon.

3
Power for Industry

A locomotive is a major investment – a lot of capital money for a company to find. The locomotive building industry grew alongside the development of the railway system itself, initially making locomotives for the main line railways until they established their own works for manufacture. As major workshops such as Swindon and Crewe established themselves, a lot of smaller builders began to fall by the way, but others diversified into locomotive export or building for the industrial customer. In Whitehaven, Tulk & Ley, who built Crampton express engines sold their premises and became Fletcher Jennings, with an eye to both light and industrial railway markets.

Many firms maintained the capacity to build for the main line railway, and indeed took on subcontracts for steam locomotives into the 1950s in some cases. The growth, decline and rebirth of the private locomotive industry is a study in itself and has filled many books and articles. The wheel has now turned full circle in 2022, with main line workshops left privatised and competing for work, and several small businesses for locomotive engineering custom. Those that have adapted have changed with the circumstances and even embraced new technology in the form of hybrid power in the example of Clayton in Derbyshire, to whom we shall return.

Not every industrial locomotive was bought new for industry. As with all types of plant and equipment, there has always been a thriving second-hand market. Very many of the pioneering locomotives of the nineteenth century were sold into further use with collieries, private lines and contractors. The famous and iconic *Rocket* itself was sold to the Brampton Railway in Cumbria where it found a new lease of life. Others such as Sans Pareil were adapted to become stationary engines, providing power for winches, sawmills or pumps before final disposal.

Dealers in second-hand locomotives addressed the need for something to push a few wagons around, and in many early cases that was all that an older engine was fit for. The famous Isaac Watt Boulton became well known for buying, repairing, and hiring old locomotives for industrial purposes, operating out of 'Boulton's Siding' alongside the Oldham branch of the Manchester, Sheffield & Lincoln Railway from 1864. The book *Chronicles of Boulton's Siding* (originally published in 1927) gives a fantastic insight into the business and the machines and illustrates what was happening in many places across the country. Dealers such as A. R. Adams in Newport, J. F. Wake of Darlington and Dunn's of Bishop Auckland show how widespread the sale, repair and hire of locomotives could be. Records of these firms reveal large numbers of locomotives, some simply passing through and others being repaired and repainted but failing to sell for many years until final disposal. Further diversity was introduced by contractors offering locomotives for hire, either simply as an individual machine, or as plant as part of a wider deal with the contractor's services as well. Civil engineers like Robert A. McAlpines had a massive fleet of locomotives, not all in use at one time, but a sign of the importance of the industrial railway in all its facets. Use of locomotives from one manufacturer of the same basic design also meant much easier maintenance due to standardisation of parts and their ability to be switched from one engine to another.

Locomotives came in all sizes and types. Four-wheel (0-4-0) and six-wheel (0-6-0) tank engines dominated the market, carrying their own coal and water supply on a single underframe. The water tanks took the form of side tanks either side of the boiler, saddle tanks over the top of the boiler, a well tank between the frames under the boiler or even pannier tanks – slung either side of the boiler but not reaching down to the running plate as in side tanks. That is not to say that tender locomotives were not used in industry – many of the earlier sales from main line to industry, like *Rocket*, were tender engines. In the North East, where some of the private lines were longer, the tradition of buying second-hand tender engines continued until the end of the nineteenth century, when larger purpose-built tank engines began to hold sway on the Lambton system. The sale of locomotives from main line companies has continued to the present day, with hundreds of steam locomotives and diesel shunters finding a new lease of life beyond the large rail companies. Some have lasted but a few months, others worked for decades, and then found a way into preservation, and it is for this reason that there are examples of both North Staffordshire Railway and Glasgow & South Western Railway locomotives preserved today. British Railways sold many tank engines to the National Coal Board in the 1950s and 1960s, and it is ironic that the two Austerity type saddle tanks that made their way to become class J94 on the national network both survive today purely because of their second life moving coal.

The last commercially working steam locomotives in Central London were former Great Western Railway pannier tank locomotives bought by London Transport from British Rail. The final ones ran into 1971, decked in the resplendent LT maroon livery, causing much distraction to commuters when operating on Underground lines large enough to take them.

No small industrial shunter, this 0-6-2 side tank was made for the North Staffordshire Railway in 1922 and sold by the London, Midland & Scottish Railway in the 1930s to the Manchester collieries. It worked until the late 1960s and survived to be part of the Foxfield Railway Museum collection back in Staffordshire.

With a working life extending into the 1950s, this small shunter from Kynochs chemical plant at Witton in Birmingham lasted much longer in industry than it did with the London & North Western Railway who built it. Currently on display at the Ribble Steam Railway in Preston, its industrial life ensured that it became a rare survivor.

4
Mass Production and One-offs

The builders ranged from small concerns who made one loco only, through to the large concerns who built for export, the home market and the main line railways. As well as these, there were the industries and works who were sufficiently well equipped and skilled to make their own locomotives – often based on something they already had experience of. The Coalbrookdale Works in Shropshire made a small batch of saddle tank locomotives which were very successful, one of which is now to be seen at Enginuity, part of the Ironbridge suite of museums, having been operational until 1959. Similarly, the Haydock Foundry made several well tank engines designed by Josiah Evans for the Haydock Collieries, and Robert Heath & Sons did similar in Staffordshire with eleven saddle tank locomotives for their coal and iron interests between 1888 and 1926. Other industries with large workshops extensively rebuilt locomotives and in some cases assembled new ones using stocks of spare parts they had, or combined components of several machines to make a new one.

Josiah Evans of Haydock made model locomotives as an apprentice, but by the 1870s was making full-size locomotives for Haydock Collieries. The 1874-built *Bellerophon* is now owned by the Vintage Carriages Trust and was operating here at the 2014 Steam Gala at Locomotion.

The morning sun catches the light on the smokebox of the now unique Robert Heath-built saddle tank *No.6* as it raises steam for a photo session at Locomotion in October 2006.

Despite these interesting local efforts, the majority of steam locomotives for industrial use were of standard designs with set specifications from well-known manufacturers. The technical specification changed little until the latter days of steam production. Engines were mainly sold by their number of wheels and cylinder size, which dictated their power output. A design could run to hundreds of production models supplied to any number of customers. Some firms stuck rigidly to one supplier; others shopped around. A customer could buy an entire fleet of one design, to help with standardisation of parts and maintenance, though that was quite a capital outlay. Each manufacturer had their own colours that they turned out their locomotives in unless the customer specified otherwise. As a result, the industrial railway scene was rather colourful, and when locomotives were clean, they could be very eye-catching indeed. As the twentieth century drew on, some collieries and steelworks added the black and yellow 'wasp' stripes to bufferbeams, saddle tanks and bunkers of locomotives to make them more visible in the gloom of their surroundings. A few, such as Corby steelworks, actually painted their locomotives completely yellow, though this did little once the soot and grime of work began to build up on the engine. On the other hand, a beautifully turned-out locomotive with a fine livery was a source of pride for its owners and crew, and while many locations operating steam into the 1970s and 1980s had filthy engines, that pride remained at several NCB sites, most notably Bold Colliery and Cadley Hill, both of whom we shall return to later in the book.

Stewarts & Lloyds tube works at Bromford Bridge near Birmingham made sure that their Avonside saddle tank was as visible as possible by 1964 – the original colours would have been subdued, but the yellow and black 'wasp' stripes helped it stand out in the industrial environment.

Cadley Hill colliery in Derbyshire kept its working steam locomotive immaculate into the 1980s. At the National Coal Mining Museum for England, Robert Stephenson & Hawthorn saddle tank *Progress* still shines on display in 2019, over thirty years since it left colliery service.

Out of all the designs, one perhaps stands out for comment more than any other, mainly because of the large numbers made – and thus the large number that have survived for preserved railway use – the Hunslet Ministry of Supply saddle tank, often simply known as the Hunslet 'Austerity'. Conceived in 1942 for war use during the Second World War, it had a design life of two years and was made to move 1,000 tons on the level. Nearly 500 were made and deployed across the UK and Europe, some making their way to North Africa. Hunslet could not deliver the locomotives fast enough, so further construction was sub-contracted to Bagnall, Barclay, Robert Stephenson and Hawthorn, Hudswell Clarke and Vulcan Foundry. At the end of hostilities, a large number of these fairly modern locomotives became surplus to requirements and made their way on to the second-hand market. The London & North Eastern Railway, about to become British Railways, bought seventy-eight, classifying them J94 and putting them to work on the main line railway. The National Coal Board, formed in 1947, saw a chance to replace many elderly locomotives across the country relatively cheaply, and many Austerities entered civilian service. This continued into the 1950s as military depots reassessed their requirements, but over 100 Austerity design saddle tank locomotives were made new for the home market, finding their way to collieries in the main, but also the East Midlands ironstone quarries. In the latter, Yorkshire Engine Company made eight for their own systems with slight design changes for their purposes. The final four were made between 1958 and 1964, the last one, Hunslet works number 3890 of 1964, being the last standard gauge steam locomotive made for home use commercially in the UK until the construction of the main line locomotive *Tornado* in the twenty-first century. As will be seen in due course, some of the last steam locomotives operating in industry in the 1980s were Hunslet Austerities, lasting almost twenty years after the end of British Rail steam use.

The Thomas the Tank Engine based on the Mid Hants Railway began life as a Hunslet Austerity saddle tank. Others of the type have been reconstructed into other locomotives, including the National Railway Museum's replica Great Western Railway broad gauge replica *Iron Duke*, which has an Austerity boiler, cylinders and other mechanical parts. Eighty remain in existence in one form or another.

After the Second World War, the Hunslet Austerity saddle tank dominated much of industry, particularly the collieries. Other industries found uses for them as well, and many were built new after the war for specific customers. This one was built for the National Coal Board but has been restored to the colours of the United Steel Company and was in use on a photographic special recreating an iron ore train at Rocks by Rail in March 2010.

Many other builders were drafted in to build Austerity locos during the Second World War. This example was made by Robert Stephenson and Hawthorn, and usually works on the Tanfield Railway. In July 2021, it was visiting the Stephenson Railway Museum, North Tyneside, not far from where it used to operate commercially.

Who were the major builders of industrial steam locomotives? Companies such as Robert Stephenson, Hawthorn Leslie, Hunslet, Bagnall, Kitson, Barclay, Peckett, Avonside, Manning Wardle and Hudswell Clarke dominated the scene, issuing catalogues, adverts and brochures to show their wares. These all made thousands of locomotives, some lasting in service many decades, beyond the life of their maker. Following the economic fortunes of the country and the wiles and abilities of their directors, not all firms survived so long, and takeovers and mergers did occur, perhaps the largest being the joining of Robert Stephenson and Company with Hawthorn Leslie, to become Robert Stephenson and Hawthorn. The distribution of the manufacturers is also interesting – there being very few builders in London or Birmingham, the latter being most surprising given the amount of heavy industry there. In a similar way, the city of Bristol having Fox Walker, Avonside and Peckett is of contrast. The largest concentration of locomotive manufacture for industry in the United Kingdom must be Leeds in West Yorkshire, with a proud heritage going back to Matthew Murray and the Blenkinsop locomotives built for the Middleton Railway. In little over a square mile, the works of Manning Wardle, Hunslet, Kitson, Hudswell Clarke, E. B. Wilson, Robert Hudson and Fowler were closely grouped – though not all operative at the same time – while not far away was the works of Thomas Green. The Hunslet Engine Company were founded in the 1860s and continued rail vehicle production until the 1990s when the business moved away from Leeds. In the area, very many features of these former works remain, including the main erecting shop and offices of the Hunslet Company, the gateposts of the Manning Wardle works and the entry arch to Wilsons. In the tarmac of Jack Lane, near the Hunslet offices, rails remain as a legacy to the locomotives that were tested and then left the site on their own wheels for the journey to the customer.

On at lease one occasion, a locomotive under test at one of the Leeds Companies ran away across Jack Lane and crashed into the workshops of their competitor across the road. There was no animosity, just a little embarrassment, and probably a bit of amusement after the event!

Left: The offices of the Hunslet Engine Company remain standing in Leeds, while track remains in the road outside part of the old works over twenty years since the last item of rolling stock was produced.

Below: Companies were very proud of their new locomotives. In the late 1940s, Robert Stephenson and Hawthorn posed *Tumulus* for a works photograph in Newcastle before it undertook the long journey to its new home, the Holborough Cement Works in Kent.

Right: A smaller builder of locomotives was Stephen Lewin & Company of Poole. Sole survivor *No.14* worked in the North East for nearly a century until the late 1960s and is now part of the Beamish Museum collection.

Below: Typical of many four-wheeled saddle tank locomotives, *Hodbarrow* is a classic on 1870s locomotive design from Hunslet of Leeds and has been restored for display by the Statfold Barn Narrow Gauge Trust in Staffordshire.

5
Departures from the Norm – the Bespoke Locomotive

While we have looked at the production of conventional steam locomotives, we cannot leave the subject without considering some of the specialist machines designed for specific purposes or locations. Made in much smaller numbers, these oddities attracted attention from the enthusiast if they survived long enough to be observed and photographed, while others remain entries in works ledgers and records only, perhaps with a snatched blurred image on the edge of a wider photograph. The first departure from the normal was different wheel arrangements, and a few eight-wheeled locomotives were made for the home market, but not in great quantities due to their weight or ability to go round curves. They were mainly for collieries where the sheer ability to pull heavy trains of coal on steep gradients was the main requirement.

Less conventional and certainly rarer was the articulated locomotive, built to give extra power and flexibility in locations where sharp curves and steep gradients abounded – almost two engines in one. An American Shay type was operated at Bilston steelworks in the Midlands, but the best-known UK locomotives were the four Beyer-Garratt type locos built by Beyer Peacock for the home market. The Beyer-Garratt was much more widely built for the export market, and thousands operated worldwide. In the UK, only the London Midland & Scottish Railway ran a small fleet of them, the London & North Eastern Railway had a single large example for helping to push trains over an incline in South Yorkshire, and then there were the four made for UK industries. The Beyer Garratt consists of two engine units with a boiler mounted centrally between them. The three parts have the ability to bend between them, giving twice the amount of power for less than the weight of two standard locomotives. The four built for industrial use all had two four-wheel power units, making them the wheel arrangement 0-4-4-0. They were all made for different users, in the copper, steel and coal industries. The last built was made in 1926 and operated into the 1960s at Baddesley Colliery in Warwickshire. By that time, *William Francis*, as it was named, had become a celebrity among railway enthusiasts who sought it out as the last operating Beyer-Garratt in the UK and a unique survivor. When taken out of service at the colliery, it was bought privately and lent to the Bressingham Steam Museum in Norfolk, to whom it now belongs. It is a source of wonder and inspiration to all who see it, for there is nothing else quite like it on the standard gauge, although narrow gauge Beyer Garratts now run on the Welsh Highland Railway in North Wales.

A larger number of specialist locomotives were the crane locomotives – steam locomotives fitted with crane jibs to give them the ability to lift and carry loads from one site on a works complex to another, quite often steelworks and shipyards. The majority of these were made by Andrew Barclay or Hawthorn Leslie and their successors, RSH. The crane fixtures were themselves powered by steam with the ability to slew, swing and lift separately to the

Industrial Beyer-Garratts were unusual in the UK. *William Francis* worked its entire life for Baddesley Colliery in Warwickshire and made a rare visit from its current home at Bressingham to the Great Garratt Gathering at Manchester in 2009.

locomotive being driven along. Versatile machines, they may have been small in number, but many lasted a long time in service. The Doxford Shipyard in Sunderland became the last bastion of these machines, running nine in total dating from 1902 to 1940 construction. The 1940 engines were actually cancelled orders from 1918, kept in stock by RSH. The locomotives had very hard lives, working in the steep gradients and confined spaces of the shipyard, but nothing bettered them until they were finally taken out of service in 1971, by which time they were worn out. Four were saved by preservation schemes, but it says much that five decades after being withdrawn none are currently operational – though Southwick on the Keighley and Worth Valley Railway is currently under repair. The other remaining crane locomotives are by Barclay with three survivors, and the unique 1902 Dubs of Glasgow example, currently based in steam at the Foxfield Railway. It goes without saying that a crane engine with overhanging jib is no use pulling passenger trains at all, and it takes a special type of enthusiast to consider investing time, effort and money into repairing one for heritage use. Yet it has been done, and *Dubsy*, as it is known, is able to demonstrate the working crane locomotive to the twenty-first century audience, almost as a steam dinosaur, but one that is very much cherished and loved – a far contrast to its working days! A final crane locomotive of less conventional appearance is a black Hawthorn 2-4-0 tank, now based at Beamish Open Air Museum in County Durham. With a normal steam locomotive underframe comprising traditional cylinders and wheels, it is a heavily built oil-fired vertical boiler steam crane about the running plate, made for steelworks use. It remains a most remarkable oddity, but we must be grateful that the foresight was had to preserve it for future generations, for otherwise, apart from photographs, we would have very little record of it ever existing.

By far the most numerous of the less conventional steam locomotives was the fireless locomotive. In essence a Thermos flask on wheels, but containing steam as well as water, these were developed in the UK during the First World War for working in munitions factories where the risk of ashes, cinders and sparks from a traditionally fired locomotive were considered too great. Charged with a supply of steam from an external source (often the factory boilers), a fireless engine could then run for several hours due to the physics in play within the steam reservoir. After the end of the war, fireless engines found favour in chemical works, oil refineries

The Foxfield Railway in Staffordshire is a haven of industrial railway heritage and is the base of this unique Dubs-built crane locomotive, which is the only working example in the UK.

and paper mills, and became a particular speciality of Barclays of Kilmarnock, being built up until the late 1950s. Being easy and clean, many lasted beyond the coal-fired locomotive in their respective industries, and the author can remember being shown the yellow fireless visible at Croda, Four Ashes, Staffordshire, from a passing train in the late 1970s. The majority were made by Andrew Barclay of Kilmarnock, with a handful from other builders. The solitary Peckett-made example is now displayed alongside the A57 Cadishead bypass in Lancashire.

At Locomotion in Shildon is a 1956-built Barclay fireless locomotive from the Imperial Paper Mills in Gravesend. It's newer than one of the diesel shunters used to move the exhibits around!

Further unconventional steam locomotives were those made by several of the traction engine manufacturers, adapting the road steam technology that they were familiar with. Aveling & Porter were foremost in the field, building engines that looked for all the world like they could be driven off down the highway. Slow but powerful, they found a niche market in the chalk pits and cement industry of the South East and their native Kent in particular. The final Aveling & Porter locomotive was made in 1926, already many years after its time, and was said to have been ordered by the manager of Holborough cement works in Kent out of sentiment. The author's grandfather knew it as 'The Puffing Billy' when he was a locomotive driver at the same works, and today it is 'The Blue Circle' at the Nene Valley Railway near Peterborough.

Fowlers of Leeds and Marshalls of Gainsborough made more traction engine locomotives, but the Sentinel Waggon Works of Shrewsbury went beyond this. Builders of high-pressure steam lorries (or 'waggons' as they always termed them), it was inevitable that they would experiment with putting this power onto the rails. Initial rebuilds and conversions of traditional locomotives with vertical boilers and twin-cylinder high-speed engines led to the company building complete locomotives with the wheels connected and driven by chains instead of rods. Sentinels continued with steam locomotive production until the late 1950s, their 100-hp and 200-hp machines being very popular and powerful pieces of equipment. Sentinels saw the writing on the wall for steam and adapted to build diesels around the same time, even converting some of the steam locos that came back in for overhaul and repair into unrecognisable diesel locomotives utilising the original steam running gear.

One could continue further into locomotives that were built for specific purposes and locations – Peckett made a very low height engine for working under a particular bridge at Courtaulds Flint works, it's now known as 'The Flying Bufferbeam' as it is so short. The extensive network at Beckton Gasworks in London had many short locos for working under the retorts and the two Bagnall saddle tanks *Judy* and *Alfred*, of low height for the port of Par in Cornwall, became the inspiration for the two characters 'Bill' and 'Ben' in Revd W. Awdry's Railway Series of story books.

Most of the Aveling & Porter traction engine locomotives were built and used in the south-east of England. *The Blue Circle* made a rare visit to County Durham in 2006 and ran for a weekend at Locomotion.

Under a railway viaduct at the Museum of Iron in Coalbrookdale is one of the early Sentinel conversions of a conventional locomotive. This began life as a saddle tank in 1873 but was rebuilt by Sentinel in 1925 to its current state.

The final flowering of the Sentinel steam locomotive was the 100-horsepower model. This example, *Frank Galbraith*, represents the type in the National Collection but is currently on loan to Streetlife Museum in Hull.

Many locomotives bore names to identify them, others were simply numbers, nicknames or nothing at all. Sites with fleets could often adopt a theme. Naming locomotives after monarchs was a popular one, or places, and business owners called engines after wives, directors, popular characters both real and fictional. Sometimes a nameplate could be almost as long as the locomotive that carried it – *Marston Thompson and Evershed No. 3* being a case in point on the Foxfield Railway. However, the ultimate must go to the colliery engine that managed the very impressive *Rothervale No. 0*.

Beckton gasworks locomotives had a unique low-slung appearance, and none were fitted with cab roofs. *No. 25* was made by Neilson of Glasgow in 1895 and is today an exhibit at Bressingham Steam Museum in Norfolk, at whose sixtieth anniversary event it was seen outside in September 2021.

The *Lady Armaghdale* was for many years painted black and part of the fleet for the Manchester Ship Canal railways. In 1963 it was sold to ICI and acquired a bright red livery and its aristocratic name. The Engine House at Highley on the Severn Valley Railway is now its home.

The Oxfordshire Ironstone Company named its steam locomotives according to the number of wheels they had. The four-wheeled engines were given female names and the six wheelers male names.

On a cold and foggy day in the early 1960s, the four-wheeled Hudswell-Clarke saddle tank *Barabel* was busy in the quarries of the Oxfordshire Ironstone Company.

6
Steam on the Wane – the Alternatives to Tradition

The serious production of internal combustion locomotives began in the years after the First World War, initially petrol-powered machines but the diesel engine soon proved suitable for use in industrial railway applications. Locomotive builders began to diversify, while other new manufacturers joined the scene having never made a railway locomotive before. Some makers stuck with steam – Peckett made just five diesels and by the time they did, it was too late to save the company. Ruston & Hornsby of Lincoln became major players with high-quality power plants in solidly made and reliable running gear and superstructures. Armstrong Whitworth led the way for diesel electric power in the early 1930s, while mechanical transmission remained a favourite for many. Cab comforts were sparse, and a diesel could be a very cold place without a firebox to keep the driver warm. The smaller Motor Rail Simplexes, with their origins in the First World War, had only a simple roof over the driver, with the elements able to whistle through. That said, they did have the convenience of being able to start at very short notice and didn't require attention all the time like a steam locomotive. Like the shunting horse though, the Simplex had limited capacity and was best suited to moving one or two wagons in a small yard. Their simplicity of use and economy won them many friends, and variations on the Simplex theme were produced for the rest of the twentieth century.

Diesel hydraulics came in to give smooth, jerk-free speed and power variations without worrying about gearboxes and clutches and became the preserve of Sentinel and later Thomas Hill, with Barclay and Hunslet joining the fray as well. Specific designs evolved for

The small Simplex internal combustion locomotives were in essence a low-maintenance shunting horse. This one worked at Berry Wiggins oil refinery in Kent and is now part of the National Collection at Locomotion.

certain sites and applications, the Hunslet six-wheeled centre cab locomotives of the mid-1960s becoming known as the 'Snibston' type, named after the coal products plant that the first two of the design were made for. Industrial design ensured that newer diesels had good all-round visibility and were ergonomically created to be user friendly for the driver. The Sentinels by 1964 had won a Capital Goods Design Award and looked stylish and modern, much more suitable for the railway image that was being projected as steam was phased out. The change was hard fought for, early Fowler and Hudswell Clarke designs having steam-engine-style chimney castings over their exhausts. Some of the latter's products also had pseudo coal bunkers on the back of the cab, and the controls were laid out like a steam locomotive. The longevity of some diesel shunters is now rivalling the steam locomotives they supplanted in many cases. A 1940s Fowler diesel was sold from preservation at the Middleton Railway in Leeds to the concrete manufacturing plant at Plasmor, Great Heck, and can be seen in operation daily by passengers on the East Coast Main Line between York and Doncaster. It is maintained in excellent mechanical and cosmetic condition, and, failing major breakdown, looks set to serve for many more years.

The National Coal Mining Museum at Caphouse Colliery near Wakefield is home to this Snibston type Hunslet diesel, displayed under the screens of the colliery.

Sentinel number 10004 is the oldest survivor of its type. It was used by the makers as a demonstrator model at several places before being sold to the Bass Brewery. Finishing as a hire locomotive in the 2000s, it can be seen at Locomotion where it is in the company of the Sheffield sewage works wagon in this picture.

Fowler and Sentinel diesel locomotives are in daily use at the Plasmor Concrete Works in Yorkshire alongside the East Coast Main Line.

Overhead wire and battery electric locomotives found a niche in locations where either electricity was plentiful, or they needed to be as clean as possible. Many power stations and tram companies ran small four-wheeled electric locos taking their power from cables above the tracks. Coke oven locomotives were often electrically powered, but the largest system using such machines was the Harton Colliery network in the North East of England. The electrified system opened in 1908, and originally employed a fleet of electric locomotives built by Siemens. The extensive network included a line which ran from Westoe Colliery to the company's Low Staiths on the River Tyne. There was also a line from Harton Colliery up to Westoe Colliery, and also a line from Boldon Colliery to the High Staiths, by the River Tyne in South Shields. The Harton Electric Railway closed in 1989. When the author and his father visited to see the railway they arrived the day after it had been converted to a conveyor for moving the coal – much less interesting! A selection of electric locomotives survives in heritage ownership around the country, but very few are in working order. One of the Harton locomotives, E4, is exhibited at the Stephenson Railway Museum, Tyne & Wear, and has been restored to run off batteries that are hidden in a coal wagon that can be pulled around by the locomotive. A further advantage of electric power was that it was instantly available and able to be operated with very little training. Maintenance costs were also greatly reduced. Yet, until the recent renaissance with Claytons, which we shall review shortly, there have been very few electric locomotives working outside mining, underground and light rail systems in recent years.

Beamish Museum is home to this 1908 Siemens electric loco from the Harton Colliery System.

Working electric locomotives are unusual in preservation; the former Spondon Power Station English Electric from 1935 was in operation under battery power at the closing event in October 2017 of the former Electric Railway Museum. It's now at the Battlefield Line in Leicestershire.

Right: Coke oven locomotives are, by nature of their duty, very tall. Preserved examples are rare. This 1979 Greenwood & Batley one represents its builder at the Middleton Railway, Leeds.

Below: The closed South Bank coke works on Teesside had two locomotives built locally in 1986 by the Hartlepool Workshops of the British Steel Corporation. Both locomotives can be seen to the left of the picture and were still on site in 2021 after the demolition of everything else in this photograph. They were both finally scrapped with the redevelopment of the site by 2022.

As with their steam counterparts, many main line diesel shunters were sold into industrial service, some being exported. The practice continues into the twenty-first century, so much so that the Industrial Railway Society's book on the subject, *Ex-BR Diesels in Industry*, is now on its eighteenth edition. Let it not be said that this was the preserve of small yard shunters alone. What became known as the Class 14, large six-wheeled diesel locomotives for short haul goods work, was rendered redundant by the Modernisation Plan, which saw the traffic it was built for vanish very soon after they were made. The National Coal Board and British Steel Corporation each bought large numbers of these locomotives to use on their larger systems in the North East and around Corby steelworks respectively – both users keeping the locomotives in operation well into the 1980s, long enough for many to make the transition to heritage railway use. A single Class 17 centre cab Bo-Bo diesel found its way to Ribble Cement in Clitheroe – not really an ideal industrial locomotive one might think, but again, it lasted in use until the early 1980s and once more was taken into preservation as a result. At Scunthorpe steelworks, a single Class 20 Bo-Bo is now stored out of use, its working life in the hard surroundings of the steel industry at an end.

The commonplace Class 03 and 08 locomotives were widespread around the UK, and while the former is almost all gone from industry now, they served for over thirty years in private hands. The Class 08 is a remarkable machine though. Diesel electric transmission makes for a smooth and controllable machine, even if visibility isn't great with the engine bay in front of the driver to full height. The oldest dates to 1952 and some 996 were made. Of those, 100 are still in use as this book was written, with many being hired to main line operators or other industrial concerns. A further eighty-two are preserved, but it is not unknown for a preserved Class 08 to make the journey back into commercial use, such is the success of this long-serving type. At nearly seventy years old, the private locomotive manufacturers have striven to produce an affordable Class 08 replacement and have yet to succeed on a widespread basis.

In 2021, the drive to decarbonise Britain's railways had reached such a point that a project to convert a Class 08 to hydrogen power was under way at the Severn Valley Railway.

Barrow Hill in Derbyshire is a working railway depot as well as a heritage site. Some of the Harry Needle Railroad Company hire fleet of Class 08 shunters are seen in 2019 during maintenance work; the company orange livery ensures that the locomotives are visible on industrial sites.

With a finite resource in the Class 08, the requirement for other locomotives in industry remains, with special needs of loading gauge, axle weight or application. While coking ovens at steelworks are very unusual applications, they needed their own locomotives to push the coke cars. So, it is also within oil refineries and steelworks in general that carefully designed locomotives find their application. Upcycling and rebuilding has extended the lives of many locomotives from the 1950s to 1970s, but even with this the hard-working environment of heavy industry has seen these machines come to the economic limit of repair. The Yorkshire Engine Company 'Janus' type was a specific machine for the steel industry, and a few remain in use, well over fifty years old, but these are becoming an exception. Large Bo-Bo diesel electrics by Hunslet, built in the 1970s, supplanted the Janus at Scunthorpe steelworks, while 1996-built Maschinenbau Kiel machines of similar design have largely taken over from the Hunslets too. Refinements such as remote control improve the efficiency and effectiveness of rail operations in an environment where 'Just In Time' delivery is the key to success and production keeping to schedule.

ICI in Derbyshire undertook an amazing rebuild of an old Avonside steam tank engine into a purpose-built diesel shunter with Rolls-Royce engine and a tall cab for extra visibility and driver comfort. It is bright yellow and wins no prizes for aesthetic charm. After laying derelict for years, it has been restored in the ICI workshops and has a new life with the Andrew Briddon collection in the county where it worked.

The Ministry of Defence settled upon a standard design of diesel shunter from Thomas Hill of Rotherham. Four were in the Graven Hill shed at Bicester depot in January 2013.

Out on the clifftop at Skinningrove in June 2020 was a Yorkshire Engine Company 0-6-0 diesel hydraulic; YEC produced a great number of locomotives for the iron and steel industry. This example has had a long and hard life.

New build locomotives are something to be looked forward to, and it's heartening to see new construction by several firms in recent years. Perhaps the highest profile currently is Clayton Equipment of Derbyshire, who have well and truly grasped the nettle of decarbonisation. They have recently made several hybrid power battery locos with small diesel engines for Port Talbot steelworks and British Nuclear Fuels at Sellafield. Elsewhere, the famous Hunslet Engine Company and all the subsidiaries that formed it, including Andrew Barclay, Greenwood & Batley and Hudswell Clarke, remains active with locomotive repair, hire and construction, most recently as part of the Ed Murray & Sons operation, which has been building up its own overhaul, repair and hire work.

Since the privatisation of the British Railway network, many shunters are owned by companies such as Murrays, mentioned above, while Rail Support Services and Harry Needle Railroad Company both operate large hire fleets. They serve both the private user and the Train Operating Companies and repairers on the main line, and it is not unusual to see locomotives move venue several times in a year according to need. An RSS, Murray or HNRC locomotive may start off at a main line depot and end up in a repair works, limestone quarry, container yard or docks having visited other sites in between. The

Clayton Equipment opened their doors in January 2020 to share the new build hybrid locomotives they were building for Tata Steel in Port Talbot. These are now in service and other locomotives to the same design are being made for other customers.

companies employ travelling fitters to maintain disparate fleets across the country. This is of course the modern incarnation of some of the old dealers, contracting or hire firms of the twentieth century, and the yards of each company often contain locomotives under repair, awaiting hire or stored pending sale or scrap – a happy hunting ground for the industrial railway enthusiast – though it must be said, in the busy commercial world, any desire to see locomotives needs to be sought in writing first with an appointment made. These are businesses who are operating on time specific deadlines, and they are unable to accommodate the casual enthusiast, notwithstanding modern safety considerations as well. This is where the Industrial Railway Society comes into its own, as it has officers who arrange visits to installations, companies and sites where industrial railways can be seen in operation or their remains viewed.

Many industrial locomotive operators had an agreement with the main line railway companies that their machines could travel on parts of the national network as long as they were registered to do so. The British Transport Commission had registration plates made up which such locomotives had to carry.

Long Marston Rail Innovation Centre at the former Long Marston Ministry of Defence depot utilises several industrial locomotives. The most interesting are perhaps the Minilok Road/Rail machines, their dual capability making them very versatile indeed.

Working at Tees Dock Terminal, *Emily* is a rebuilt Andrew Barclay diesel on hire from LH Group Services.

T. J. Thomson were a major scrap processor in Stockton until 2016, and most of their traffic went by rail. Operating a fleet of Thomas Hill shunters, the working examples became hire locomotives for Ed Murray when the scrapyard closed.

7
Rails for All Reasons – Wagons, Track and Ropes

While most systems serving industry were – and are – of the standard gauge, there were exceptions. These were mainly for special applications in specific industries or for use on isolated systems where the connection to a main line railway did not matter. Chapelcross nuclear power station is one example that used a standard design of Ruston & Hornsby diesel shunter but built to 5 foot 4 inch gauge to allow the safe transport of nuclear flasks on-site. Likewise, the internal steel moving system of Swan-Hunter in Newcastle had no locomotives, but self-propelled trolleys to move steel plate were of larger gauge to accommodate the size of material being moved. In North Wales, the Port Dinorwic Dry Dock Company ran a steam crane of 7 foot gauge in its yard, while a little further to the west, the Holyhead Breakwater Company operated an isolated system built to the full Brunel 7 foot and ¼ inch gauge. This line was later supplanted by a standard gauge system, but at least one of its steam locomotives found a new life shipped out to the Azores to work for several more decades. It and a sister locomotive are now preserved as a result of their long life, another pair of amazing survivors saved by their industrial career. At the other end of the spectrum, the Lee Moor Tramway on Dartmoor ran two Peckett locomotives of 4 foot 6 inch gauge – almost standard gauge, and of a design standard to the company. This made the tramway technically narrow gauge, but not really in concept and execution. Below this, the next largest was the Padarn Railway again engaged with moving slate from the Dinorwic quarries on 4-foot-gauge transporter wagons but below this one moves into the very definite narrow gauge railway, covered in the author's companion book *Narrow Gauge Locomotives*.

Moving from gauge, one examines the track itself, the very bed upon which all railways are based. Once the principle of flanged wheel on edge rail had been settled on, the technology quickly spread nationally. A small quantity of plateways remained into the twentieth century, but these were few and far between. Later plateway locomotives could be – and often were – converted into conventionally wheeled locomotives and continued their working lives. Dr Michael Lewis, he of the definition of a railway, has written extensively and informatively on steam on the Sirhowy Tramroad and previously on the Penydarren Tramway, both built as plateways. On most industrial systems, the track of conventional railways has followed main line practice with either bullhead or flat bottom rail on wooden sleepers. Specialist contractors grew up providing track materials for private sidings or could even install a system. There are still several permanent way contractors now, for the industrial railways of the United Kingdom still require track maintenance or construction. A number of these contractors run their own locomotives and rolling stock too, to assist with projects and contracts. The full evolution of railway track is a subject often shied away from by historians, the notable exception being the late Andrew Dow, whose book *The Railway* is recommended. It takes the design and implementation of railways in a comprehensive and understandable way and includes sections on early track and private networks. Any preconceptions about industrial railways being bucolic byways are dispelled when one sees pictures of the trackwork at Beckton Gasworks for example – a system complete with its own signalling and telecommunications as well. Later, the Stewarts & Lloyds ironstone network around Corby also had colour light signals on its main lines to and from the steelworks. Certainly, there were overgrown lines with poor track in many places, but on a large scale where production and meeting deadlines was important, the track was maintained on a main line basis – the ironstone lines having their own permanent way teams and wagons. The major dock facilities of Port of London, Port of Bristol, Mersey Docks & Harbour Board and the Manchester Ship Canal were also noteworthy for being massive systems with very complex and organised infrastructure and administration.

Complex industrial railway systems can run on many miles of track. Scunthorpe steelworks was operating over 110 miles of railway in 2021; the rail trips run for visitors covering about 35 miles in an afternoon.

The Causey waggonway in County Durham has a replica section of wooden railway and waggon to mark its location and purpose, not far from the current Tanfield Railway.

Chaldron waggons were synonymous in the North East for the movement of coal, and four different designs are displayed at Locomotion in the Soho shed. Closest to the camera is an 1826 example from Cramlington colliery.

Rolling stock could fill several books alone. The Industrial Railway Society's *Industrial Wagons: An Introduction* is well worth seeking out, for there are as many types of wagons as there are industries. The humble wooden or steel open wagon abounded in their thousands for what were often called 'internal user wagons', that is to say that they were only operated on the industrial lines alone and not allowed out on to the national network. Tank wagons carried a cornucopia of liquids, some hazardous, others not – chemicals, food products, oils and powders, if it could be moved by rail it was. Wagons could carry hot ingots, heavy castings, or long girders – sometimes being nothing more than basic trolleys that could be pushed or pulled by locomotives. In Sunderland at the Doxford shipyard, the crane engines were accompanied by vehicles that allowed components and steel plate to be moved with ease around the yard without worrying about whether they would fit on the main line railway.

More specialist wagons came in where the loads required different handling techniques, and the side tipper came into its own. Initial wooden ones became known as the Manchester Ship Canal type, for many were used on that contract. In essence they were the forerunner of the dump truck, carting spoil and loose materials round civil engineering projects and construction sites – the latter including reservoirs, dams, and main line railway contracts such as the Great Central Railway construction or the widening of the Great Western Railway main line into Birmingham. A progression became the steel-bodied 'vee' tipper wagon, used in several industries including coal and sewage. One of the last survivors is now preserved at Locomotion in Shildon, a reminder of the once extensive rail systems that many of our major cities had in sewage treatment works. A cast plate fitted to the side advises of where the wagon may or may not run on main line track.

One of the once ubiquitous wooden side tipping wagons was displayed at Rocks by Rail. Fortunately as the museum has developed, it has been moved under cover and awaits restoration.

Specific purposes required special wagons, even if they were a simple steel box on wheels. This iron ore tippler forms part of the exhibits at Rocks by Rail.

At the other end of the scale, the wagons of the iron and steel industry were massive, both in construction and the quantity of material they were required to carry. Heavy industry required heavy rolling stock and the ultimate is the torpedo wagon, built to carry molten iron from the blast furnace to steelmaking plant. These have a capacity of 300 tons of iron and the heat radiating from them is palpable when they pass by, either empty or loaded. A lid is placed on to contain the liquid metal using electromagnetic cranes – the whole operation is awe-inspiring to say the least. In a similar way, the by product of ironmaking, the waste material, slag, is tapped and run off from the iron into ladles mounted on rail underframes. These are not lidded, and the ladles are then taken elsewhere in the site and the slag tipped – a spectacular operation, particularly at night. The empty wagons are then returned for the same process, which takes place several times a day. Although no slag ladles are preserved on heritage railways or museums, a few are retained for posterity at either sites of former steelworks or at operational locations – Consett, Teeside and Scunthorpe being but three locations. All are where the wagons are statically displayed, the Scunthorpe one being mounted on a track in the tipping position, where simulated slag is being poured from the ladle – and it is lit at night, giving a visual impression of the tipping process without the attendant heat and hazard.

The rope-worked railway grew from the early nineteenth century in the North East, but remained in operation in Cumbria until the 1980s. Created initially due to the inability of steam locomotives to climb gradients, the inclined railway continued where steep gradients made locomotive haulage impractical despite improvements in locomotive technology. The Bowes Railway in the North East became a famous survivor due to its lasting into the 1970s and featuring in a colour film *Bowes Line* documenting a day in its life. After closure, it became the first industrial site to become a Scheduled Ancient Monument and is focussed around two winding houses and the Springwell workshops complex. Now in heritage use, it has been a preserved railway in the past and is now a community heritage initiative with railway operation just one of its activities. The rope operation is currently not working, though it is to be hoped that this unique feature is part of the future for what is a site of national significance.

The industrial railway was ubiquitous, and with many small applications such as timber yards, clay pits and brickworks not using locomotives, their existence was often overlooked. Evidence of many of these railways can be found on old Ordnance Survey maps. Railways

The headquarters of the Appleby-Frodingham Railway Preservation Society within Scunthorpe steelworks is home to a very special wagon for carrying steel mill rolls.

Above: At the other end of the spectrum at Scunthorpe steelworks is one of the torpedo wagons for carrying iron and steel around the plant. Their construction is massive.

Left: On Teeside, a slag ladle is displayed on an industrial estate near to the site of a former works.

The slag ladle gate guardian at Scunthorpe has a vivid depiction of a slag pour, which lights up at night, reminding all who drive past of the very elemental processes that take place within the plant.

Above: In January 2012, a demonstration of capstan and rope shunting was taking place in the Springwell complex of the Bowes Railway near Gateshead.

Below: A Barclay saddle tank demonstrates how much industrial atmosphere the Bowes Railway can give, a world apart to the usual heritage railway environment of the branch line, but deeply significant.

Above: At the end of the day, the fire is thrown out at Springwell before the Barclay saddle tank is put to bed in the locomotive shed of the current Bowes Railway.

Left: The steam crane was one of the largest used industrial railway vehicles, often operating in locations where no other vehicle was present. This rare survivor built by Isles of Stanningley in Leeds is part of the display at Middleton Railway.

were seemingly used everywhere to move materials, often carrying simple but robust trolleys in shipyards, steelworks and nuclear power stations. As noted previously, when the author visited Swan Hunter's shipyard on the River Tyne in 2002, large flat wagons were used for transporting steel plate within the welding shops.

The industrial railway was not always the sole preserve of trains moving goods and commodities. On larger networks or systems of lines belonging to one company, passenger and pay trains were operated. Sometimes these consisted of old goods vans with benches in or cast-off main line carriages stripped of their finery but with basic seats and a roof, enough for a few miles on a colliery track. Most of these trains, sometimes known as Paddy Trains, were operated on colliery lines – a number being in South Wales or the North East, but other industrial concerns carried passengers too, either on a VIP basis or similarly transporting employees. The pay trains were employed on a larger system on a single site usually, such as a chemical or engineering works, and its arrival once a week was eagerly awaited by employees.

The Tanfield Railway runs as a former industrial railway serving the coal industry. It has no main line locomotives, and the carriages are often repurposed main line ones fitted out as if they were used on workers' trains. The picture here at Andrew's House station with Robert Stephenson locomotive *Twizell* is entirely believable.

8

Rise and Fall? The Industrial Railway in Recent Years

The decline and rise of the industrial railway could be said to have happened over the last forty to fifty years. Mainline railways moved from individual wagons of goods to block handling of traffic or containerisation. Trainload freight became the normal thing and many private sidings closed as their businesses went over to road transport. After the privatisation of British Rail, the drive to bring freight back to the railways through companies such as English, Welsh and Scottish Railways saw a degree of success. While the coal industry was on the way out, other heavy industries such as cement and steel production and processing continued to use rail traffic, and specialist goods such as nuclear fuel ensured that industrial railways continued in those businesses, and indeed expanded in many cases. The rise of hire locomotive fleets grew as did the use of the industrial railway in major construction contracts.

The Channel Tunnel was built with industrial railways of both standard and narrow gauges, and even used some diesel locomotives brought in from preserved railways. There have been several occasions when a preserved locomotive has been bought to go back into industry, and quite often then returned to preservation a second time. In London, regular travellers in and out of Paddington station were afforded a good view of the contractors' locomotives and rolling stock working on the Crossrail project. Most industrial railways are and were not historically quite so visible. It's perhaps that air of elusiveness and special nature that gave me the interest in them in the first place. To a child growing up in the 1970s when the main line railway was all blue and grey, the bright colours and different designs of the industrial locomotive brought a variety unknown, and to see such a thing on a private siding or in a yard was a highlight of any rail trip for me. As rail traffic continues to grow, the distribution centre, or rail hub, has become a new application of the industrial railway in the twenty-first century.

Regular travellers on the East Coast Main Line Railway are able to spot several industrial locomotives en route between Edinburgh and London. At Great Heck in Yorkshire, the Plasmor concrete plant has a Fowler diesel shunter that was at one time preserved on the Middleton Railway in Leeds but has since been sold back into revenue earning service, making it one of the older machines still in everyday commercial use.

Despite the gradual modernisation of the rail network, the steam locomotive continued in industrial use long after the end of steam on the national network. The largest outposts were the National Coal Board and the Central Electricity Generating Board, with other

January 2013 saw a typical train of vans and supplies in operation on the Bicester Military Railway in Oxfordshire.

This Andrew Barclay diesel was built for the British Army on the Rhine but lives a new life working modern rolling stock at Long Marston Rail Innovation Centre, where it found itself an unexpected attraction at the 2021 RailLive event.

While *Doug Tottman* is no longer in industry, the battery electric locomotive is beginning to see a renaissance. This example was converted from an overhead wire machine and worked at Heysham nuclear power station in Lancashire.

Although rail traffic has ceased at Lackenby Steelworks, some of the locomotive fleet are stored outside the modern locomotive shed and workshop. There remains hope that while they remain in good condition, the possibility of rail operations in the future is there.

oddments keeping steam through tradition or sentimentality well into the 1980s. Bold Colliery in Lancashire even sent a locomotive to the cavalcade celebrating the 150th anniversary of the Liverpool & Manchester Railway in 1980, which is probably where the author's interest in industrial railways was piqued. Castle Donington power station is widely accepted as being the last user commercially around 1992. Other notable users were Crossley Evans scrapyard in Shipley, finishing in 1984, the NCB in South Wales in 1985, and Cadley Hill colliery in Leicestershire in 1988. The latter kept steam going as the manager was a steam enthusiast, and the fleet was always maintained in fine condition, making the location a must visit for the steam fan in the 1980s. At Sellafield plant in the late 1980s when we visited on the British Nuclear Fuels tour bus, we passed their Peckett steam loco sitting on standby. You can imagine my anguish at being told photography was not allowed on the plant! Fireless locomotives also remained at some power stations and chemical plants until the 1990s.

Redundant railways and industry have always provided a ready source of scrap metal. T. J. Thomson of Stockton were massive scrap processors for the best part of fifty years. They bought locomotives, dealt and sold those which could be said to have had a degree of life left in them and broke up the no-hopers. A significant quantity of locomotives went through their hands, and they had their own fleet of internal user diesels to move scrap wagons and rolling stock. A busy yard with no public access, good viewing of activities and incumbents of the site could be had until the yard closed from an adjacent mound of earth. Crossleys of Shipley were one of the last users of steam when a locomotive they bought was repaired and used to shunt the yard in the 1980s. Still rail connected, Crossleys yard plays host to five diesel locomotives to this day: two Rustons are quietly returning to nature in bushes alongside the main line, while another three of various makes await a return of scrap to rail traffic that may or may not come. Elsewhere in Yorkshire, CF Booths of Rotherham remain very active in rolling stock recycling and pretty much scrapped all the locomotives from the Yorkshire coalfield in the 1980s and 1990s. As with Thompson's, useful locos were again sold on, and a couple of industrials are retained as yard shunters.

Even now, some steam locomotives cling on to life in scrapyards – there are four Andrew Barclay saddle tanks in the yard of Thomas Muir in Kirkcaldy. Until a few years ago, an Avonside saddle tank was buried under a pile of scrap in the yard of Jose K. Holt Gordon in Chequerbent, near Bolton. Withdrawn from service in 1966, it was pulled out in the 1980s and stood near the yard gate until 2014 when preserved and finally taken off site. Surviving for nearly fifty years in a scrapyard, it is a remarkable relic. So many more locomotives, steam, diesel and electric, have ended their days in such yards, like so much other plant and machinery, to be recycled within a matter of days or weeks. Even those on preserved lines have not always been safe, some couple of dozen preserved industrial steam locos have been scrapped and many more diesels. One or two unfortunate lines have even seen locomotives, either in whole or part, stolen for scrap. Another problem of theft of parts has rendered many projects either longer in term or unviable. However, the enthusiasm remains undimmed, and a good number of museums, centres and railways are built on the theme of industrial and independent railways, or use industrial rolling stock, and you can learn more about these in the next chapter.

Locomotives at the end of their useful life are only so much scrap metal in industry, just like any other piece of plant. These two Fowler diesels await their fate at Allen Rowland, Tyseley, Birmingham, in the 1980s.

The well-known scrapyard of T. J. Thomson in Stockton had a long line of diesel shunters. Some were stored pending resale, others joined the growing piles of scrap around them, but they provided huge interest to the industrial railway enthusiast.

At Scunthorpe steelworks, discarded locomotives – particularly of obsolete types such as the Yorkshire Engine Company *Janus* – provide spare parts for other machines still in operation.

In 2022, there are still a quartet of steam locomotives in Thomas Muir's scrapyard in Kirkcaldy. All are Andrew Barclay saddle tanks and are a sight to behold, having all come from Fife collieries during the 1960s and 1970s.

9

Get Involved – the Interest of Industry

For many years, the stalwarts have been the Industrial Railway Society and Industrial Locomotive Society. Both have their origins in the 1930s and 1940s, the Industrial Locomotive Society beginning in 1937 as the Industrial and Road Locomotive Society, the two separating out ten years later, and both are still going strong. The Industrial Railway Society was initially the Birmingham Locomotive Club Industrial Locomotive Information Section, formed in 1949 to cater for the growing interest in non-mainline operations across the country. By the mid-1960s it had become the Industrial Railway Society and was publishing handbooks of locomotive fleets past and present, for the enthusiast to see what was beyond the national network. Interest grew at the end of main line steam as the enthusiast sought out further working locomotives, and now the IRS continues to thrive, studying historic matters as well as recording the contemporary scene. Visits are organised to industrial locations and a vibrant publishing activity has seen a new series of county handbooks and specialist subject titles, including rope haulage, industrial locomotive sheds, rolling stock and former British Rail diesel locomotives sold into industry. Between the ILS and the IRS, record keeping is assiduous and membership well recommended.

The industrial railway interest extends to buildings and operations as well. At Eastriggs Ministry of Defence Depot, the locomotive shed was home to both standard and narrow gauge locomotives.

Even in the twenty-first century, gems are to be found. This Andrew Barclay shunter from 1942 is said to have seen duty on D-Day and is now a treasured pet at the Long Marston Rail Innovation Centre where it made a real contrast to the state-of-the-art rolling stock at RailLive in 2019.

The first view many will have of an industrial locomotive. In this case a mobile phone photograph of a Hunslet shunter at Oxwellmains Cement Works alongside the East Coast Main Line at Dunbar.

The Birmingham Locomotive Club, which became the Industrial Railway Society, organised a visit to Hams Hall Power Station in February 1964, where two of the large Robert Stephenson & Hawthorn locomotives were seen on shed.

Many enthusiasts came across industrial locomotives while seeking main line engines in the first case. It was certainly the case for my father, who came across this Peckett saddle tank at Cheltenham Gas Works after looking at former Great Western locos in Gloucester.

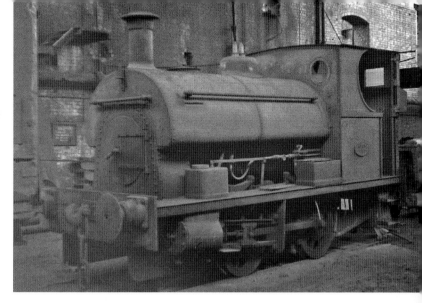

The National Railway Museum in York is home to *Bauxite*, built in 1874 and a museum piece since 1947, reminding nearly a million visitors a year of the importance of the industrial railway in the story of UK railways.

The preservation of industrial locomotives has been an activity for many years. The first privately preserved engine outside of public museums was *Bauxite*, a small Black Hawthorn saddle tank from the 1874. preserved by the North Eastern Engineering & Historical Society in 1947 and presented to the Science Museum in London. It's now on display at the National Railway Museum in York and is shown as withdrawn and conserved rather than restored to immaculate condition. As locomotives were recognised as historically significant and the enthusiast interest grew, many more made their way to museums, and then to heritage railways. Societies and trusts were formed specifically to look after certain engines, such as the Warwickshire Industrial Locomotive Trust, which has two locomotives, *The Lady Armaghdale* and *Warwickshire* in its care on the Severn Valley Railway.

While many industrial engines found new lives on heritage railways, a number were placed on public display on plinths or put in playgrounds as glorified playthings. Most of these have now moved into active heritage roles, but some remain on street corners or continue to engage youngsters who want to play at train drivers. The author's hometown of Leamington Spa at one point in the 1980s had two industrial locos in separate parks, one a Bagnall Austerity type and the other a former British Rail Class 03 diesel shunter.

In the 1980s, we found Bagnall saddle tank *Cherwell* as a climbing frame in a Daventry playground. Far from unique, safety concerns have seen most playground locos relocated in the decades since.

Another form of preservation is the plinthed for posterity Robert Stephenson and Hawthorn *Husky* diesel preserved outside the offices of AV Dawson in Middlesbrough.

The Pilling Pig preserved outside a Lancashire holiday park represents a long-gone light railway but is a 1955-built Hudswell Clarke saddle tank, which spent all its working life in the South Wales collieries. Industrial locomotives pretending to be something they aren't is also a common phenomenon.

For a short time, Fowler diesel *Fluff* was an exhibit at the Vintage Vehicles Shildon lorry museum. Since 2012 it has been at the Ribble Steam Railway in Preston where it is now under restoration.

In terms of heritage or preserved railways, while many schemes began operations with industrial locomotives, the lure of the larger main line machine has seen many smaller engines laid aside. A few lines have remained true to their origins, but in the main this is because they are based on former industrial lines or systems. Foxfield, Bowes, Chasewater, Tanfield and the Middleton Railway are all former colliery railways and retain a particular charm of their own, several running coal trains for display. In Yorkshire, the Embsay & Bolton Abbey Railway continues to use mainly industrial engines, with a mixture of ancient coaches and more recent British Railways Mark 1 stock. The Ribble Steam Railway in Preston has a marvellous collection of industrial locomotives, but also supplements their heritage activities in the museum in Preston Docks with commercially running bitumen trains with their own small fleet of Sentinel diesel shunters. All these lines and locations are always ready and willing to see new members and volunteers join their ranks, whether it is as an armchair supporter or to someone with an interest in active restoration, operation, or research. As time passes, most of the railways are becoming more active at telling their own historical stories, with interpretation panels, visitor orientation centres and small specialist museums attached to the railway.

The historic Middleton Railway in Leeds has a marvellous museum facility called the Engine House where it tells the story of Leeds locomotive building. *Mary* is the oldest standard gauge Hudswell-Clarke diesel locomotive in existence.

In Staffordshire, the Chasewater Railway has become a home to a collection of brewery railway locomotives and rolling stock. This Baguley diesel was once part of the Bass brewery fleet.

Marley Hill locomotive shed on the Tanfield Railway is full of atmosphere and is one of the oldest continuously used railway buildings in the world.

Some people have small model railways in their garden. In Buckinghamshire, David Buck has Peckett *Hornpipe*, another loco with family connections through Holborough Cement Works. It's the ultimate garden railway and great fun!

Museums are traditionally more of a repository for artefacts for interpretation and study, but some combine elements of operation, as well as conservation. Colliery railways are represented by the National Coal Mining Museum for England and Big Pit in South Wales. Other industries are represented at the National Brewing Centre in Burton upon Trent, while the Museum of Scottish Railways has a fine selection of items from various Scottish industries. In Britain's smallest county of Rutland, Rocks by Rail celebrates the vanished industry of ironstone extraction for iron and steel production. It includes a reconstructed quarry face with dragline excavators and quarry train days when demonstrations of loading are given. Not every preservation scheme has been a success, however. Chatterley Whitfield colliery, Market Overton ironstone railways and Snibston Colliery are examples that have all sadly closed in their heritage form, although statutory protection has been afforded to the buildings of the two collieries. Several other museums, both those run by trusts or local authorities, include a locomotive or two or a display on industrial railways of the region or subject that they cover.

As with many other parts of the railway interest, there is a large amount of activity in the craft of modelling industrial railways. Until recently, this was very much the preserve of people who were willing to make the model locomotives and structures themselves, either from scratch or from using kits of specific types of vehicles or building. In the last decade, mainstream manufacturers of model railways such as Hornby, Bachmann and Dapol have begun to make what is known as 'ready to run' models of industrial locomotives, and a myriad of smaller retailers and companies have also entered the market. It's now possible to buy well over a dozen models of steam and diesel industrial locomotives in the popular oo gauge, while there are even more kits of some of the more obscure or esoteric models available. For a time, both Hornby and Bachmann had ready-made colliery buildings and headgears available in oo scale, while for further detailed models Wrightscale in Scotland made a full etched brass headgear kit based on Cefn Coed colliery in South Wales. In both smaller and larger scales, it's possible to model all aspects of industrial railways, both ancient and modern. Should you wish something larger, the model engineering sizes have several designs of industrial locomotive available, while Maxitrak in Kent make and sell kits and ready to run live steam Hunslet Austerity models in 5 inch gauge – which you can drive and ride behind.

Chatterley Whitfield colliery may have gone as a museum, but this photo from 1990 shows how much of an industrial feel it had. The locomotive is a Yorkshire Engine Company saddle tank and now at Rocks by Rail in Rutland.

Snibston Museum in Coalville was on a colliery site and was also home to this amazing machine – a Brush-built saddle tank, which was once owned by the Great Western Railway, then sold to Berry Wiggins in Kent where it was converted to burn oil. When the museum closed, the locomotive was lent to Mountsorrel Heritage Centre a few miles away.

Ruston & Hornsby of Lincoln made hundreds of diesel shunters, very solid and dependable machines in a range of power sizes and wheel arrangements. One of the 165DS type was a mainstay of the now closed Electric Railway Museum, seen working on the final day in October 2017.

Rocks by Rail near Cottesmore in Rutland has many original ironstone industry features as well as the rolling stock. With the help of sponsors, it has also recreated an ironstone quarry face with excavator and operating demonstrations are given on open days.

During a photographic charter in March 2010, visiting Peckett saddle tank No. 2000 works a typical iron ore train along the line at Rocks by Rail – preservation can be very good at recreating long-lost scenes.

Markham of Chesterfield made a very small number of industrial tank engines. It's very appropriate that the sole survivor, *Gladys*, is displayed locally at the Midland Railway, Butterley.

Railway publishing has seen hundreds of books produced, from illustrated photo albums to in-depth studies of specific lines, systems, industries or types and manufacture of locomotive. So many have been published over the best part of sixty years that it would be hard to mention anything specific, though the Industrial Railway Society regional handbooks are a good starting place, along with the magisterial nine-part series by the late Eric Tonks on the Ironstone Quarries of the Midlands. The *IRS Bulletin* and journal are also regular sources of news, information, and historic research on aspects of these railways. The Industrial Locomotive Society's quarterly *The Industrial Locomotive* is full of well-researched historical articles and notes, often including old adverts for locomotives being sold, providing much inspiration for further investigation into sites, makers and owners. On the high street, *Railway Bylines* is a magazine devoted to the byways of Britain's railways and includes much industrial content.

Earlier in the book, it was noted how it can be difficult to view a full-on operating industrial railway system, be it a small siding or two or a major industrial complex with all the attendant hazards. Apart from the orgnaised visits of the Industrial Railway Society, there is one other location that stands out. The Appleby Frodingham Railway Society offer tours of Scunthorpe steelworks by train. In the author's humble opinion, the experience of this is the ultimate train ride in the UK, dodging in and out of steel production traffic and taking the train up to the blast furnace high line as far as possible. In an afternoon, the tour train attempts to travel as many of the 115 miles of steelworks rail system that it can, and no two tours are the same. Seeing the full process of a working steelworks is an awe-inspiring activity and an assault of the senses! Close to this comes preservation of industrial railways on their original sites – either as features such as Gloucester Docks and Bristol Docks or in total as per Chatham Docks, which must be unique as a heritage railway that does not have any passenger rolling stock or carry passengers. But then, every industrial railway is unique.

A view from the brake van of the blast furnace complex at Scunthorpe steelworks during a tour. A very special experience indeed and much recommended.

Above: Steel billets on the move at Scunthorpe behind one of the Hunslet diesels in the fleet. An amazing spectacle and good to see such use of rail in heavy industry in the twenty-first century.

Below: The industrial railway interest can be very personal. Peckett *Teddy* is owned by a good friend of the author, Gary Boyd-Hope, but neither of us would have thought when we met in our teens that we would both be enjoying his engine in July 2016 at my workplace, Locomotion.

My father's family connections to Kent meant that in the 1960s he was able to visit relations and the cement works that provided a living to his own father before the Second World War. We saw *Tumulus* as a new engine in its works photograph in a previous chapter. Here it is at Holborough Works towards the end of its career.

A personal favourite. In the 1950s, the Steel Company of Wales commissioned three Bagnall saddle tanks with all modern details, roller bearings, piston valves and much more. Two finished their working lives with British Leyland at Longbridge car works, but it was a delight to see one of them returned to its original condition now at the Stephenson Railway Museum in July 2021.